Favorite Poems

Favorite Poems

124 Poems with Spiritual Power

Compiled by Al Bryant

ZONDERVAN PUBLISHING HOUSE

OF THE ZONDERVAN CORPORATION
GRAND RAPIDS, MICHIGAN 49506

FAVORITE POEMS

Copyright 1957 by Zondervan Publishing House
Grand Rapids, Michigan

Twenty-first printing   1977
ISBN 0-310-22072-6

Printed in the United States of America

CONTENTS

FOREWORD

The poems in this compilation were selected not so much on the basis of their literary excellence as upon their strongly heart-warming quality. Many of them are the compiler's own favorites. Others have proved themselves favorites among Christians who particularly enjoy poetry. We are indebted to Mr. Paul Meyers, "First Mate Bob" of the famous Haven of Rest Radio Program, and the Rev. Wilbur Nelson of the Morning Chapel Hour for their observations as to those poems which elicited greatest praise and comment from their radio listening audience.

The compiler has particularly enjoyed his work in collecting this group of well-known and not-so-well-known poems. Each poem has been of personal blessing and challenge — and it is hoped that they will be a source of blessing to scores of readers around the world.

It was difficult to separate these beautiful pieces of Christian literature into "hard and fast" categories — but an attempt has been made to categorize these poems as an added convenience for those who wish to use them in a public ministry (they are also indexed by title and author, where known). It is in the hope that they will prove a blessing wherever they are used, whether in the pulpit or during the private devotional hour, that these poems are presented to the Christian reading public.

THE COMPILER

Grand Rapids, Michigan

ACKNOWLEDGMENTS

Heart-felt appreciation is due the Evangelical Publishers of Toronto, Canada, for permission to use the copyrighted poems of Annie Johnson Flint. Grateful acknowledgment is also expressed to the original publishers of the other poems in the compilation — the poems of the well known Martha Snell Nicholson, Bob Jones, Jr., Horatius Bonar, Avis B. Christiansen, Oswald J. Smith, Amy Carmichael and Frances Ridley Havergal, to mention just a few.

We wish to express appreciation, too, to the great poets of the past and present who made this book possible through the work of their dedicated and talented pens.

MY OLD BIBLE

Though the cover is worn,
And the pages are torn,
And though places bear traces of tears,
Yet more precious than gold
Is this Book worn and old,
That can shatter and scatter my fears.

This old Book is my guide,
'Tis a friend by my side,
It will lighten and brighten my way;
And each promise I find
Soothes and gladdens the mind,
As I read it and heed it each day.

To this Book I will cling,
Of its worth I will sing,
Though great losses and crosses be mine;
For I cannot despair,
Though surrounded by care,
While possessing this blessing divine.

IT MEANS JUST WHAT IT SAYS

There are some who believe the Bible,
    And some who believe a part;
Some who trust with a reservation,
    And some with all the heart.
But I know that its every promise
    Is firm and true always;
It is tried as the precious silver,
    And it means just what it says.

It assures me of salvation
    Thro' Jesus' precious Blood,
For the souls that will trust His mercy,
    And yield themselves to God.
And I claim for myself the promise
    And just begin to praise,
For it says I am saved by trusting,
    And I trust just as it says.

And it tells me there is cleansing,
    From every secret sin,
And a great and full salvation
    To keep the heart within;
And I take Him in His fullness,
    With all His glorious grace,
For He says it is mine for taking,
    And I take just what He says.

And it tells me He will heal me,
  And hear my feeblest cry,
And that all His royal bounty,
  Will all my need supply.
And I seem to know no better,
  Than to trust Him all my ways,
For He says I may trust Him fully,
  And I trust just as He says.

Let me hearken to all His precepts,
  And instantly obey;
Let me run to perform His bidding,
  Whatever He may say.
Let me cherish His least commandment,
  And walk in all His ways;
Let me always obey my Master
  And do just what He says.

It is strange we trust each other,
  And only doubt our Lord;
We will take the words of mortals
  And yet distrust His Word;
But oh, what a light and glory,
  Would shine o'er all our days,
If we always would remember
  He means just what He says.

MY COMPANION

When quiet in my room I sit,
  Thy Book be my companion still;
My joy Thy sayings to repeat,
  Talk o'er the records of Thy will,
And search the oracles divine,
  Till every heartfelt word is mine.

—*Charles Wesley*

OUR GUIDING LIGHT

If we could plunge to the depths of truth
  And grasp the whole rich story,
Our souls would rise to Paradise
  Enraptured by its glory.

What boundless wealth lies in this Book
  Peculiar as a treasure.
Its brilliant rays shine on our ways
  Availing without measure.

Oh, Word divine! Oh, Book sublime!
  Oh, Wisdom so transcending!
We look to Thee, we cling to Thee,
  For guiding light unending.

—*S. F. Logsdon*

THE WORLD'S BIBLE

Christ has no hands but our hands
  To do His work today;
He has no feet but our feet
  To lead men in His way;
He has no tongue but our tongue
  To tell men how He died;
He has no help but our help
  To bring them to His side.

We are the only Bible
  The careless world will read;
We are the sinner's gospel,
  We are the scoffer's creed;
We are the Lord's last message,
  Given in deed and word;
What if the type is crooked?
  What if the print is blurred?

What if our hands are busy
  With other work than His?
What if our feet are walking
  Where sin's allurement is?
What if our tongues are speaking
  Of things His lips would spurn?
How can we hope to help Him
  And hasten His return? —*Annie Johnson Flint*

THE SACRED BOOK

I love the sacred Book of God,
  No other can its place supply;
It points me to the saints' abode,
  And bids me from destruction fly.

Sweet Book! In thee my eyes discern
  The image of my absent Lord;
From thy instructive page I learn
  The joys His presence will afford.

But while I'm here thou shalt supply
  His place, and tell me of His love;
I'll read with faith's discerning eye,
  And thus partake of joys above.

—*Thomas Kelly*

HIS WORD IS POWERFUL

His Word is like fire consuming,
  His Word is a hammer to break;
His Word is a sword with two edges.
  His Word like a lamp you can take.

His Word is against the false prophets,
  His Word is opposed to all sin;
His Word will endure forever,
  His Word will the victory win.

His Word is both written and living,
  His Word will outlive sword and pen;
His Word is His eternal edict,
  His Word: — it is yea and amen.

                              —*H. H. Savage*

GOD'S TREASURE

There is a Treasure,
Rich beyond measure,
  Offered to mortals today;
Some folk despise it,
Some criticize it,
  Some would explain it away.

Some never read it,
Some never heed it,
  Some say "It's long had its day";
Some people prize it,
And he who tries it
  Finds it his comfort and stay.

God gave this Treasure,
Rich beyond measure,
  His Word, we call it today.
Let us believe it,
Gladly receive it,
  Read, mark, and learn to obey.

                              —*A. M. N.*

15

IF I BUT READ

The Lord I love went on ahead
To make a home for me. He said
He would come back again, and He —
Oh, gracious love — He wrote to me!
He knew I was so weak and blind
And foolish that I could not find
The road alone. He told me things
That all earth's wise men, and its kings,
Have never guessed, yet I foreknow
If I but read His Word. And, oh,
Such depths of love on every sheet!
My soul is trembling at His feet.
What would He think of me
If when I saw Him I should say;
"I was too busy every day
To read what Thou didst write to me;
I really hadn't time for Thee!"

—*Martha Snell Nicholson*

CHALLENGE...

A SINGLE STITCH

One stitch dropped as the weaver drove
  His nimble shuttle to and fro,
In and out, beneath, above,
  Till the pattern seemed to bud and grow
As if the fairies had helping been;
One small stitch which could scarce be seen,
But the one stitch dropped pulled the next stitch out,
And a weak place grew in the fabric stout;
And the perfect pattern was marred for aye
By the one small stitch that was dropped that day.

One small life in God's great plan,
  How futile it seems as the ages roll,
Do what it may or strive how it can
  To alter the sweep of the infinite whole!
A single stitch in an endless web,
A drop in the ocean's flood and ebb!
But the pattern is rent where the stitch is lost,
Or marred where the tangled threads have crossed;
And each life that fails of its true intent
Mars the perfect plan that its Master meant.

                             —Susan Coolidge

IF JESUS CAME TO YOUR HOUSE

If Jesus came to your house to spend a day or two,
If He came unexpectedly, I wonder what you'd do.
Oh, I know you'd give your nicest room to such an
      honored Guest,
And all the food you'd serve to Him would be the
      very best —
And you would keep assuring Him you're glad to have
      Him there,
That serving Him in your home is joy beyond compare!
But when you saw Him coming, would you meet Him
      at the door,
With arms outstretched in welcome to your Heavenly
      Visitor?
Or would you have to change your clothes before you
      let Him in,
Or hide some magazines and put the Bible where
      they'd been?
Would you turn off the radio and hope He hadn't
      heard —
And wish you hadn't uttered that last, loud, hasty
      word?
Would you hide your worldly music and put some
      hymn books out?
Could you let Jesus walk right in, or would you rush
      about?
And I wonder — if the Saviour spent a day of two
      with you —

Would you go right on doing the things you always
    do?
Would you keep right on saying the things you always
    say?
Would life for you continue as it does from day to day?
Would your family conversation keep up its usual
    pace?
And would you find it hard each meal to say a table
    grace?
Would you sing the songs you always sing and read
    the books you read,
And let Him know the things on which your mind and
    spirit feed?
Would you take Jesus with you everywhere you'd
    planned to go,
Or would you, maybe, change your plans for just a
    day or so?
Would you be glad to have Him meet your very closest
    friends,
Or would you hope they'd stay away until His visit
    ends?
Would you be glad to have Him stay forever on and
    on,
Or would you sigh with great relief when He at last
    was gone?
It might be interesting to know the things that you
    would do
If Jesus came in person to spend some time with you.

IF THE LORD SHOULD COME

If the Lord should come in the morning
    As I go about my work,
The little things and the quiet things
    That a servant cannot shirk,
Though nobody ever sees them,
    And only the dear Lord cares
That they always are done in the light of the sun,
    Would He take me unawares?

If the Lord came hither at evening,
    In the fragrant dew and dusk,
When the world drops off its mantle
    Of daylight like a husk,
And flowers in wonderful beauty
    And we fold our hands and rest,
Would His touch of my hand, His low command,
    Bring me unhoped-for zest?

Why do I ask and question?
    He is ever coming to me,
Morning and noon and evening,
    If I have but eyes to see.
And the daily load grows lighter,
    The daily cares grow sweet,
For the Master is near, the Master is here,
    I have only to sit at His feet.

—J. R. Miller

NO TIME

I knelt to pray, but not for long,
   I had too much to do,
Must hurry off and get to work,
   For bills would soon be due.

And so I said, a hurried prayer,
   Jumped up from off my knees;
My Christian duty now was done,
   My soul could be at ease.

All through the day I had no time
   To speak a word of cheer,
No time to speak of Christ to friends—
   They'd laugh at me, I feared.

No time, no time, too much to do —
   That was my constant cry;
No time to give to those in need —
   At last 'twas time to die.

And when before the Lord I came,
   I stood with downcast eyes,
Within His hands He held a Book,
   It was the "Book of Life."

God looked into His Book and said,
   "Your name I cannot find,
I once was going to write it down,
   But never found the time."

"WHO IS ON THE LORD'S SIDE?"

Who is on the Lord's side?
  Who will bid the world good-by?
Who will stand forth bravely,
  Saying, Master, here am I?"

Who will offer service,
  Join the ranks of marching host?
Who will take all orders
  From the precious Holy Ghost?

Who will give God glory,
  Take the hidden, humble place?
Who will wield God's weapon
  Of redeeming love and grace?

Who is on the Lord's side?
  Who will lift the banner high?
Hear the call that's sounding!
  Answer, comrade, "Here am I"!
                              —*Grace B. Renfrow*

SCARRED

The shame He suffered left its brand
In gaping wound in either hand;
Sin's penalty He deigned to meet
Has torn and scarred His blessed feet;
The condemnation by Him borne
Marred His brow with print of thorn.
Trespass and guilt for which He died
Have marked Him with a riven side.

Mine was the shame, the penalty:
The sin was mine; it was for me
He felt the nails, the thorns, the spear.
For love of me the scars appear
In hands and feet and side and brow.
Beholding them I can but bow
Myself a living sacrifice
To Him who paid so dear a price.

—*Bob Jones, Jr.*

SAVED, BUT —

I am saved, but is self buried?
  Is my one, my only aim,
Just to honor Christ my Saviour,
  Just to glorify His Name?

I am saved, but is my home life
  What the Lord would have it be?
Is it seen in every action,
  Jesus has control of me?

I am saved, but am I doing,
  Everything that I can do,
That the dying souls around me,
  May be brought to Jesus, too?

I am saved, but could I gladly,
  Lord, leave all and follow Thee;
If Thou callest can I answer,
  Here am I, send me, send me?

O MASTER, LET ME WALK WITH THEE

O Master, let me walk with Thee
In lowly paths of service free;
Tell me Thy secret; help me bear
The strain of toil, the fret of care.

Help me the slow of heart to move
By some clear, winning word of love;
Teach me the wayward feet to stay,
And guide them in the homeward way.

Teach me Thy patience; still with Thee
In closer, dearer company,
In work that keeps faith sweet and strong,
In trust that triumphs over wrong.

In hope that sends a shining ray
Far down the future's broad'ning way;
In peace that only Thou canst give,
With Thee, O Master, let me live.

—*Washington Gladden*

PROVE THE DOCTRINE

So let our lips and lives express
The holy Gospel we profess,
So let our words and virtues shine
To prove the doctrine all divine.

FIRST THINGS FIRST

No time, no time for study,
  To meditate and pray —
And yet much time for **"doing"**
  In a fleshly, worldly way.

No time for things Eternal
  But much for things of earth,
The things important set aside
  For things of little worth.

Some things, 'tis true, are needful
  But first things must come first;
And what displaces God's own Word
  Of God it shall be cursed.
  —*M. E. H.*

SLAVES

They are slaves who fear to speak
For the fallen and the weak;
They are slaves who will not choose
Hatred, scoffing and abuse,
Rather than in silence shrink
From the truth they needs must think;
They are slaves who dare not be
In the right with two or three.
  —*James Russell Lowell*

LEAD ME TO CALVARY

King of my life, I crown Thee now,
  Thine shall the glory be;
Lest I forget Thy thorn-crowned brow,
  Lead me to Calvary.

Show me the tomb where Thou wast laid,
  Tenderly mourned and wept;
Angels in robes of light arrayed
  Guarded Thee whilst Thou slept.

Let me like Mary, thro' the gloom,
  Come with a gift to Thee;
Show to me now the empty tomb,
  Lead me to Calvary.

May I be willing, Lord, to bear
  Daily my cross for Thee;
Even Thy cup of grief to share,
  Thou has borne all for me.
                    — *Jennie Evelyn Hussey*

BREATHE ON ME, BREATH OF GOD

Breathe on me, Breath of God,
  Fill me with life anew,
That I may love what Thou dost love,
  And do what Thou wouldst do.

Breathe on me, Breath of God,
   Until my heart is pure,
Until with Thee I will one will,
   To do or to endure.

Breathe on me, Breath of God,
   Till I am wholly Thine,
Till all this earthly part of me,
   Glows with Thy fire divine.

Breathe on me, Breath of God,
   So shall I never die,
But live with Thee the perfect life
   Of Thine eternity.

—*Edwin Hatch*

WATCH AND PRAY

Christian, seek not yet repose,
   Cast thy dreams of ease away;
Thou art in the midst of foes;
   Watch and pray.

Gird thy heavenly armor on,
   Wear it ever night and day;
Near thee lurks the evil one;
   Watch and pray.

Hear the victors who o'ercame;
   Still they watch each warrior's way;
All with one deep voice exclaim,
   "Watch and pray."

—*Charlotte Elliott*

THINK IT OVER

I'll go where You want me to go, dear Lord;
   Real service is what I desire;
I'll say what You want me to say, dear Lord—
   But don't ask me to sing in the choir.

I'll say what You want me to say, dear Lord;
   I like to see things come to pass;
But don't ask me to teach girls and boys, dear Lord—
   I'd rather just stay in my class.

I'll do what You want me to do, dear Lord;
   I yearn for the Kingdom to thrive;
I'll give You my nickels and dimes, dear Lord—
   But please don't ask me to tithe.

I'll go where You want me to go, dear Lord;
   I'll say what You want me to say;
I'm busy just now with myself, dear Lord—
   I'll help You some other day.

BE TRUE THYSELF

Thou must be true thyself
   If thou the truth wouldst teach;
Thy soul must overflow if thou
   Another's soul wouldst reach,
It needs the overflow of heart
   To give the lips full speech.

Think truly, and thy thoughts
    Shall the world's famine feed;
Speak truly, and each word of thine
    Shall be a fruitful seed;
Live truly, and thy life shall be
    A great and noble creed.
                    —*Horatius Bonar*

THE DAY BEFORE

Some time some ordinary day will come,
A busy day, like this, filled to the brim
With ordinary tasks — perhaps so full
That we have little care or thought for Him.

And there will be no hint from silent skies,
No sign, no clash of cymbals, roll of drums—
And yet that ordinary day will be
The very day before our Lord returns!

The day before we lay our burdens down,
And learn instead the strange feel of a crown!
The day before all grieving will be past,
And all our tears be wiped away at last!

O child of God, awake and work and pray!
That ordinary day might be — today!
Make ready all thine house—tomorrow's sun
May dawn upon the Kingdom of God's Son.

CALL BACK

If you have gone a little way ahead of me, call back;
It will cheer my heart and help my feet along the
stony track.
And, if the light of my faith is dim, because the oil
is low,
You will guide my lagging steps as wearily I go.
Call back and tell me He went with you into the storm.
Call back and say He kept you when the forest's roots
were torn,
And that, when the heavens thundered and the earth-
quake shook the hill,
He bore you up and held you where the very air was
still.

Friend of mine, call back and tell me, for I cannot see
your face;
They say it glows with triumph and your feet bound
in the race.
But there are mists between us, and my spirit eyes
are dim,
And I cannot see the glory, though I long for word of
Him.
But if you'll say He heard you when your prayer was
but a cry,
And if you'll say He saw you through the night's sin-
darkened sky;
If you have gone a little way ahead, friend of mine,
call back;
It will cheer my heart and help my feet along the
stony track.

TO ANY DADDY

There are little eyes upon you, and they're watching
night and day;

There are little ears that quickly take in every word
you say;

There are little hands all eager to do everything you
do,

And a little boy who's dreaming of the day he'll be
like you.

You're the little fellow's idol, you're the wisest of the
wise;

In his little mind about you no suspicions ever rise;

He believes in you devoutly, holds that all you say
and do

He will say and do in your way when he's grown up
like you.

There's a wide-eyed little fellow who believes you're
always right,

And his ears are always open and he watches day
and night,

You are setting an example every day in all you do,

For the little boy who's waiting to grow up to be like
you.

ARE ALL THE CHILDREN IN?

I think ofttimes as the night draws nigh
   Of an old house on the hill,
Of a yard all wide and blossom-starred
   Where the children played at will.
And when the night at last came down,
   Hushing the merry din,
Mother would look around and ask,
   "Are all the children in?"

'Tis many and many a year since then,
   And the old house on the hill
No longer echoes to childish feet,
   And the yard is still, so still.
But I see it all, as the shadows creep,
   And though many the years have been
Since then, I can hear mother ask,
   "Are all the children in?"

I wonder if when the shadows fall
   On the last short, earthly day,
When we say good-bye to the world outside,
   All tired with our childish play,
When we step out into the Other Land
   Where mother so long has been,
Will we hear her ask, just as of old,
   "Are all the children in?"

SOMEONE IS FOLLOWING YOU

Don't forget that day by day
Someone is following you;
Be careful what you say,
Be careful what you do.

Don't forget as you go along
Someone is following you;
Watch to avoid the wrong.
Watch the path you pursue.

God help you this truth to see;
Someone is following you;
Be strong! His witness be,
Be strong! Live always true.

—*Clifford Lewis*

I SHALL NOT PASS THIS WAY AGAIN

Through this toilsome world, alas!
Once and only once I pass;
If a kindness I may show,
If a good deed I may do
To a suffering fellow man,
Let me do it while I can.
No delay, for it is plain
I shall not pass this way again.

WHAT THEN?

When the great plants of our cities
   Have turned out their last finished work;
When our merchants have sold out their last
      yard of silk
   And dismissed the tired clerk;
When our banks have raked in their last dollar
   And paid their last dividend,
When the Judge of the world says, "Close for
      the night,"
   And asks for a balance—what then?

When the choirs have sung their last anthem,
   And the preacher has read his last prayer;
When the people have heard their last sermon
   And the song has died on the air;
When the Bible lies closed on the altar,
   And the pews are all empty of men,
And each one stands facing their record,
   And the Great Book is open—what then?

When the actors have played their last drama,
  And the mimic has made his last fun;
When the film has flashed its last picture,
  And the billboard has displayed its last run;
When the crowds seeking pleasure have vanished
  And gone out into darkness again;
When the trumpet of ages is sounded
  And we stand up before Him—what then?

When the bugles' last call sinks into silence,
  And the long marching columns stand still;
When the captain has given his last orders.
  And they have captured the last fort and hill;
When the flag has been furled from the masthead,
  And the wounded afield have checked in,
And the world that rejected its Saviour
  Is asked for a reason — what then?

FILL ME NOW

Hover o'er me, Holy Spirit,
  Bathe my trembling heart and brow;
Fill me with Thy hallowed presence,
  Come, O come and fill me now.

Thou canst fill me, gracious Spirit,
  Though I cannot tell Thee how;
But I need Thee, greatly need Thee,
  Come, O come and fill me now.

I am weakness, full of weakness,
  At Thy sacred feet I bow;
Blest, divine, eternal Spirit,
  Fill with pow'r, and fill me now.

Cleanse and comfort, bless and save me,
  Bathe, O bathe my heart and brow;
Thou art comforting and saving,
  Thou art sweetly filling now.

—*E. R. Stokes*

"YOU TOLD ME OF JESUS"

When the voice of the Master is calling
  And the gates into Heaven unfold,
And the saints of all ages are gathering
  And are thronging the city of gold;
How my heart shall o'erflow with the rapture
  If a brother shall greet me and say,
"You pointed my footsteps to Heaven.
  You told me of Jesus the Way."

COMFORT...

SECURITY

More secure is no one ever
Than the loved ones of the Saviour;
Not yon star, on high abiding,
Nor the bird in home-nest hiding.

God His own doth tend and nourish,
In His holy courts they flourish;
Like a father kind He spares them,
In His loving arms He bears them.

Neither life nor death can ever
From the Lord His children sever;
For His love and deep compassion
Comfort them in tribulation.

Little flock, to joy then yield thee!
Jacob's God will ever shield thee;
Rest secure with this Defender,
At His will all foes surrender.

What He takes or what He gives us
Shows the Father's love so precious;
We may trust His purpose wholly—
'Tis His children's welfare solely.

—Lina Sandell

WHAT GOD HATH PROMISED

God hath not promised
  Skies always blue,
Flower-strewn pathways
  All our lives through;
God hath not promised
  Sun without rain,
Joy without sorrow,
  Peace without pain.

God hath not promised
  We shall not know
Toil and temptation,
  Trouble and woe;
He hath not told us
  We shall not bear
Many a burden,
  Many a care.

God hath not promised
  Smooth roads and wide,
Swift, easy travel,
  Needing no guide;
Never a mountain,
  Rocky and steep,
Never a river
  Turgid and deep.

But God **hath** promised
   Strength for the day,
Rest for the labor,
   Light for the way,
Grace for the trials,
   Help from above,
Unfailing sympathy,
   Undying love.

—*Annie Johnson Flint*

(Copyright by Evangelical Publishers, Toronto, Canada.)

HE WILL NEVER FAIL

Can the sun forget its rising?
   Can the stars forget to shine?
Can the moon forget its duty?
   Then can God His will resign.

Can the sea forget to roar?
   Can the waves cease and be still?
Can the waters stop giving?
   Then God can forget His will.

Can the skies above be measured?
   Can the foes of God prevail?
Can a man earth's structure fathom?
   Then God's promises can fail.

—*H. H. Savage*

WONDERFUL IS MY SAVIOUR

Wonderful is my Saviour,
Wondrous the peace in my soul,
Since I at the fountain of cleansing
Was redeemed and fully made whole.
Wondrous the joy He bestoweth,
Since I from my guilt am free;
But the wonder of wonders forever,
Is the love of my Saviour for me.

Wonderful is His power,
Who holdeth the earth in His hands.
Angels in Heaven adore Him,
And bow at His holy commands.
Wonderful is His glory,
Great is His majesty,
But the wonder of wonders forever
Is the love of my Saviour for me.

Wonderful are the heavens,
The work which my Father hath wrought.
Sun, moon, stars He hath fashioned,
Whose daily course changeth not.
Wonderful is all nature,
Mountains and plains and sea,
But the wonder of wonders forever
Is the love of my Saviour for me.

—*Avis B. Christiansen*

RULES FOR DAILY LIFE

Begin the day with God;
   Kneel down to Him in prayer;
Lift up thy heart to His abode
   And seek His love to share.

Open the Book of God,
   And read a portion there;
That it may hallow all thy thoughts
   And sweeten all thy care.

Go through the day with God,
   Whate'er thy work may be.
Where'er thou art — at home, abroad,
   He still is near to thee.

Converse in mind with God;
   Thy spirit heavenward raise;
Acknowledge every good bestowed,
   And offer grateful praise.

Conclude the day with God;
   Thy sins to Him confess.
Trust in the Lord's atoning blood,
   And plead His righteousness.

Lie down at night with God,
   Who gives His servants sleep;
And when thou tread'st the vale of **death**
   He will thee guard and keep.

OUR ROCK

If life's pleasures cheer thee,
　Give them not thy heart,
Lest the gifts ensnare thee
　From thy God to part;
His praises speak, His favor seek,
　Fix there thy hope's foundation,
Love Him, and He shall ever be
　The Rock of thy salvation.

If sorrow e'er befall thee,
　Painful though it be,
Let not fear appall thee;
　To thy Saviour flee;
He, ever near, thy prayer will hear,
　And calm thy perturbation;
The waves of woe shall ne'er o'erflow
　The Rock of thy salvation.

Death shall never harm thee,
　Shrink not from his blow,
For thy God shall arm thee
　And victory bestow;
For death shall bring to thee no sting,
　The grave no desolation;
'Tis gain to die with Jesus nigh—
　The Rock of thy salvation.

—Francis Scott Key

COMPANIONSHIP

No distant Lord have I,
   Loving afar to be;
Made flesh for me, He cannot rest
   Unless He rests in me.

Brother in joy and pain,
   Bone of my bone was He,
Now—intimacy closer still,
   He dwells Himself in me.

I need not journey far
   This dearest Friend to see;
Companionship is always mine,
   He makes His home with me.

I envy not the Twelve,
   Nearer to me is He;
The life He once lived here on earth
   He lives again in me.

Ascended now to God,
   My witness there to be,
His witness here am I because
   His Spirit dwells in me.

O glorious Son of God,
   Incarnate Deity,
I shall forever be with Thee
   Because Thou art with me.

                    —Maltbie D. Babcock

THE SAVIOUR CAN SOLVE EVERY PROBLEM

The Saviour can lift every burden,
  The heavy as well as the light;
His strength is made perfect in weakness,
  In Him there is power and might.

The Saviour can bear every sorrow,
  In Him there is comfort and rest;
No matter how great the affliction,
  He only permits what is best.

The Saviour can strengthen the weary,
  His grace is sufficient for all;
He knows every step of the pathway,
  And listens to hear when we call.

The Saviour can break sin's dominion,
  The victory He won long ago;
In Him there is freedom from bondage,
  He's able to conquer the foe.

The Saviour can satisfy fully
  The heart that the world cannot fill;
His presence will sanctify wholly
  The soul that is yielded and still.

The Saviour can solve every problem,
  The tangles of life can undo;
There is nothing too hard for Jesus
  There is nothing that He cannot do.
                    —*Oswald J. Smith*

MY FRIEND

I've found a Friend whose equal
This world has never known,
And for His loss no treasure
Of earth could e'er atone.
He bids me bring my burdens,
However, great or small,
To Him in full assurance
That He will bear them all.

I've found a Friend whose equal
This world has never known,
Whose Blood for my transgressions
So freely doth atone.
He bids me come for cleansing
To His dear pierced side,
Where e'en for me there floweth
The precious crimson tide.

I've found a Friend whose equal
This world has never known;
He understands my trials,
And counts them as His own.
He comforts me in sorrow,
He cheers me when oppressed,
He takes my griefs and burdens,
And gives me peace and rest.

KEPT EVERY MOMENT

If Christ is mine, then all is mine,
  And more than angels know;
Both present things, and things to come,
  And grace and glory too.

If He is mine, let friends forsake,
  And earthly comforts flee;
He the Dispenser of all good,
  Is more than all to me.

Let Christ assure me He is mine;
  I nothing want beside.
My soul shall at the fountain live
  When all the streams are dried.
                              —*John Roberts*

THE NAME OF JESUS

How sweet the name of Jesus sounds
  In a believer's ear;
It sooths his sorrows, heals his wounds,
  And drives away his fear.

It makes the wounded spirit whole,
  And calms the troubled breast;
'Tis manna to the hungry soul,
  And to the weary rest.
                              —*John Newton*

A REFUGE AND PRESENT HELP

God is the refuge of His saints,
    When storms of sharp distress invade;
Ere we can offer our complaints,
    Behold Him present with His aid.
                                —*Isaac Watts*

BUT WE SEE JESUS

I don't look back, God knows the fruitless efforts,
    The wasted hours, the sinning, the regrets,
I leave them all with Him who blots the record,
    And mercifully forgives, and then forgets.

I don't look forward, God sees all the future,
    The road that, short or long, will lead me home,
And He will face with me its every trial,
    And bear for me the burdens that may come.

But I look up — into the face of Jesus,
    For there my heart can rest, my fears are stilled,
And there is joy, and love, and light for darkness,
    And perfect peace, and every hope fulfilled.
                                —*Annie Johnson Flint*

(Copyright by Evangelical Publishers, Toronto, Canada.)

MOMENT BY MOMENT

Never a trial that He is not there;
Never a burden that He doth not bear;
Never a sorrow that He doth not share;
Moment by moment, I'm under His care.

Never a heart-ache, and never a groan,
Never a tear-drop, and never a moan,
Never a danger but there, on the throne,
Moment by moment, He thinks of His own.

Never a weakness that He doth not feel;
Never a sickness that He cannot heal.
Moment by moment, in woe or in weal,
Jesus, my Saviour, abides with me still.
                              —*Daniel W. Whittle*

A SURE REFUGE

Safe in Jehovah's keeping,
  Safe in temptation's hour,
Safe in the midst of perils,
  Kept by Almighty power.
Safe when the tempest rages,
  Safe though the night be long;
E'en when my sky is darkest
  God is my strength and song.
                              —*Sir Robert Anderson*

THE NEW LEAF

He came to my desk with quivering lip;
The lesson was done.
"Have you a new leaf for me, dear Teacher?
I have spoiled this one!"
I took his leaf, all soiled and blotted,
And gave him a new one, all unspotted,
Then into his tired heart I smiled:
"Do better now, my child."

I went to the throne with trembling heart;
The year was done.
"Have you a new year for me, dear Master?
I have spoiled this one!"
He took my year, all soiled and blotted,
And gave me a new one, all unspotted,
Then into my tired heart He smiled:
"Do better now, my child!"

PROTECTED

Hidden in the hollow of His blessed hand,
Never foe can follow, never traitor stand;
Not a surge of worry, not a shade of care,
Not a blast of hurry moves the spirit there.

GOD'S MERCY

There's a wideness in God's mercy
  Like the wideness of the sea;
There's a kindness in His justice
  Which is more than liberty,
There is welcome for the sinner,
  And more graces for the good;
There is mercy with the Saviour;
  There is healing in His blood.

There is no place where earth's sorrows
  Are more felt than up in heaven;
There is no place where earth's failings
  Have such kindly judgment given.
There is plentiful redemption
  In the blood that has been shed;
There is joy for all the members
  In the sorrows of the Head.

For the love of God is broader
  Than the measure of man's mind,
And the heart of the Eternal
  Is most wonderfully kind.
If our love were but more simple,
  We should take Him at His word,
And our lives would be all sunshine
  In the sweetness of our Lord.

                    —*Frederick William Faber*

CONSECRATION...

ABIDE WITH ME

Abide with me: fast falls the eventide;
The darkness deepens; Lord with me abide:
When other helpers fail and comforts flee,
Help of the helpless, O abide with me!

Swift to its close ebbs out life's little day;
Earth's joys grow dim, its glories pass away;
Change and decay in all around I see;
O Thou who changest not, abide with me!

I need Thy presence every passing hour;
What but Thy grace can foil the tempter's power?
Who like Thyself my guide and stay can be?
Through cloud and sunshine, O abide with me!

Hold Thou Thy word before my closing eyes;
Shine through the gloom, and point me to the skies:
Heaven's morning breaks, and earth's vain shadows flee—
In life, in death, O Lord, abide with me!

—H. F. Lyte

THE THREEFOLD WORK

Three things the Master hath to do,
  And we who serve Him here below
And long to see His Kingdom come,
  May pray or give or go.

He needs them all — the open hand,
  The willing feet, the asking heart—
To work together and to weave
  The threefold cord that shall not part.

Nor shall the giver count his gift
  As greater than the worker's need,
Nor he in turn his service boast
  Above the prayers that voice his need.

Not all can go, nor all can give
  To arm the others for the fray;
But young or old or rich or poor,
  Or strong or weak — we all can pray.

Pray that the full hands open wide
  To speed the message on its way,
That those who hear the call may go
  And pray—that other hearts may pray.

                              —*Annie Johnson Flint*

HIS PLAN FOR ME

When I stand at the judgment seat of Christ,
  And He shows me His plan for me,
The plan of my life as it might have been
  Had He had His way — and I see
How I blocked Him here, and checked Him there,
  And I would not yield my will—
Will there be grief in my Saviour's eyes,
  Grief, though He loves me still?
He would have me rich, and I stand there poor,
  Stripped of all but His grace,
While memory runs like a hunted thing
  Down the paths I cannot retrace.
Then my desolate heart will well-nigh break
  With the tears that I cannot shed;
I shall cover my face with my empty hands,
  I shall bow my uncrowned head.
Lord of the years that are left to me,
  I give them to Thy hand;
Take me and break me, and mould me
  To the pattern Thou hast planned!

                    —*Martha Snell Nicholson*

When thou has thanked thy God
  for every blessing sent,
What time will then remain
  for murmurs or lament?

WHOLLY THE LORD'S

My whole though broken heart, O Lord,
  From henceforth shall be Thine;
And here I do my vow record—
  This hand, these words are mine;
All that I have, without reserve,
  I offer here to Thee;
Thy will and honor all shall serve
  That Thou bestow'st on me.

All that exceptions save I lose;
  All that I lose I save;
The treasures of Thy love I choose,
  And Thou art all I crave.
My God, thou hast my heart and hand;
  I all to thee resign;
I'll ever to this covenant stand,
  Though flesh hereat repine.

I know that Thou wast willing first,
  And then drew my consent;
Having thus loved me at the worst
  Thou wilt not now repent.
Now I have quit all self-pretense,
  Take charge of what's thine own:
My life, my health, and my defense,
  Now lie on Thee alone.

                              —*Richard Baxter*

MORE HOLINESS

More holiness give me;
　　More strivings within,
More patience in suffering,
　　More sorrow for sin.
More faith in my Saviour,
　　More sense of His care,
More joy in His service,
　　More purpose in prayer.

More gratitude give me,
　　More trust in the Lord,
More pride in His glory,
　　More hope in His Word.
More tears for His sorrows,
　　More pain at His grief,
More meekness in trial,
　　More praise for relief.

More purity give me,
　　More strength to o'ercome,
More freedom from earth-stains,
　　More longings for home;
More fit for the kingdom,
　　More used I would be,
More blessed and holy—
　　More, Saviour, like thee.
　　　　　　　　—*Philip Paul Bliss*

THE MASTER'S TOUCH

In the still air the music lies unheard;
  In the rough marble beauty hides unseen;
To wake the music and the beauty, needs
  The master's touch, the sculptor's chisel keen.

Great Master, touch us with Thy skillful hand!
  Let not the music that is in us die;
Great Sculptor, hew and polish us, nor let,
  Hidden and lost, Thy form within us lie!

Spare not the stroke! do with us as Thou wilt,
  Let there be nought unfinished, broken, marred!
Complete Thy purpose, that we may become
  The perfect image, O our God and Lord!
                                        —*Horatius Bonar*

IT'S THE FLAME THAT IS IMPORTANT

His lamp am I. To shine where He shall say,
And lamps are not for sunny rooms,
Nor for the light of day.
And as sometimes a flame we find,
Clear, shining through the night,
So bright, we do not see the lamp
But only see the light,
So may I shine — His light the flame —
That men may glorify His name.
                                        —*Annie Johnson Flint*

(Copyright by Evangelical Publishers, Toronto, Canada.)

TAKE THOU, O LORD

Take Thou my voice, O Lord, I give it gladly,
  Let it proclaim to all the world Thy love;
Take Thou my tongue and may it glorify Thee,
  Until at last I sing Thy praise above.

Take Thou my hands and let them do Thy bidding,
  Use them, dear Lord, to work for Thee alone;
Take Thou my feet, and train them for Thy service,
  May they be swift to make Thy message known.

Take Thou my heart and consecrate it wholly,
  May it be true no matter what betide;
Take Thou my life, it must be Thine forever
  For I would turn away from all beside.

Take Thou my love, O Lord, and consecrate it,
  Burn out the dross and make it all Thine own;
Save me from self and all of earth's ambitions
  Till self has died and Thou dost reign alone.

                              —*Oswald J. Smith*

THE HAPPY HOME

Happy the home when God is there,
  And love fills every breast,
Where one their wish, and one their prayer,
  And one their heavenly rest.

THE RIDICULOUS OPTIMIST

There was once a man who smiled
   Because the day was bright,
   Because he slept at night,
   Because God gave him sight
To gaze upon his child;
   Because his little one,
   Could leap and laugh and run;
   Because the distant sun
Smiled on the earth he smiled.

He smiled because the sky
   Was high above his head,
   Because the rose was red,
   Because the past was dead!
He never wondered why
   The Lord had blundered so
   That all things have to go
   The wrong way, here below
The over-arching sky.

He toiled, and still was glad
   Because the air was free,
   Because he loved, and she
   That claimed his love and he
Shared all the joys they had!
   Because the grasses grew,
   Because the sweet winds blew,
   Because that he could hew
And hammer, he was glad.

Because he lived he smiled,
   And did not look ahead
   With bitterness or dread,
   But nightly sought his bed
As calmly as a child.
   And people called him mad
   For being always glad
   With such things as he had,
And shook their heads and smiled.
       —*Samuel Ellsworth Kiser*

ADORATION

I love my God, but with no love of mine,
   For I have none to give;
I love Thee, Lord, but all the love is Thine
   For by Thy love I live.
I am as nothing, and rejoice to be
Emptied and lost and swallowed up in Thee.

Thou, Lord, alone art all Thy children need.
   And there is none beside;
From Thee the streams of blessedness proceed,
   In Thee the blest abide—
Fountain of life and all-abounding grace,
Our source, our center, and our dwelling place.

       —*Madame Guyon*

DELIVER ME

From prayer that asks that I may be
Sheltered from winds that beat on Thee,
From fearing when I should aspire,
From faltering when I should climb higher,
From silken self, O Captain, free
Thy soldier who would follow Thee.

From subtle love of softening things,
From easy choices, weakenings
(Not thus are spirits fortified,
Not this way went the Crucified),
From all that dims Thy Calvary,
O Lamb of God, deliver me.

Give me the love that leads the way,
The faith that nothing can dismay,
The hope no disappointments tire,
The passion that will burn like fire;
Let me not sink to be a clod;
Make me Thy fuel, Flame of God.

—*Amy Carmichael*

LIFE

Life is a burden; bear it.
Life is a duty; dare it.
Life is a thorn crown; wear it.

Though it break your heart in twain,
Though the burden crush you down,
Close your lips and hide the pain;
    First the cross and then the crown.

TRUE WISDOM

True wisdom is in leaning
  On Jesus Christ, our Lord;
True wisdom is in trusting
  His own life-giving word;
True wisdom is in living
  Near Jesus every day;
True wisdom is in walking
  Where He shall lead the way.

HIS STRENGTH

And, as the path of duty is made plain,
May grace be given that I may walk therein,
  Not like the hireling, for his selfish gain,
With backward glances and reluctant tread,
Making a merit of his coward dread—
  But, cheerful, in the light around me thrown,
  Walking as one to pleasant service led;
  Doing God's will as if it were my own
Yet trusting not in mine, but in His strength alone!
          —*John Greenleaf Whittier*

THE IMAGE OF GOD

Father of eternal grace,
  Glorify Thyself in me;
Sweetly beaming in my face
  May the world Thine image see.

Happy only in Thy love,
  Poor, unfriended, or unknown;
Fix my thought on things above;
  Stay my heart on Thee alone.

To Thy gracious will resign'd—
  All Thy will by me be done;
Give me, Lord, the perfect mind
  Of Thy well-beloved Son.

Counting gain and glory loss,
  May I tread the path He trod;
Die with Jesus on the Cross,
  Rise with Him to live with God.
                    —*Charles Wesley*

EMPTY HANDS

One by one He took them from me,
  All the things I valued most;
Until I was empty-handed,
  Every glittering toy was lost.

And I walked earth's highways, grieving,
  In my rage and poverty,
Till I heard His voice inviting,
  "Lift your empty hands to me."

So I held my hands toward Heaven
  And He filled them with a store
Of His own transcendent riches
  Until they could hold no more.

And at last I comprehended,
  With my stupid mind and dull,
That God could not pour His riches
  Into hands already full!

—Martha Snell Nicholson

THE TOUCH OF THE MASTER'S HAND

'Twas battered and scarred, and the auctioneer
  Thought it scarcely worth his while
To waste much time on the old violin,
  But he held it up with a smile;
"What am I bidden, good folk?" he cried,
  "Who'll start the bidding for me?
A dollar—one dollar—then two, only two—
  Two dollars, and who'll make it three?
Going for three"—but no—
  From the room far back, a gray-haired man
Came forward and picked up the bow;
  Then wiping the dust from the old violin,
And tightening the loosened strings,
  He played a melody pure and sweet
  As a caroling angel sings.

The music ceased and the auctioneer,
  With a voice that was quiet and low,
Said, "Now what am I bid for the old violin?"
  And he held it up with the bow;
"A thousand dollars—and who'll make it two?
  Two thousand and who'll make it three?
Three thousand once—three thousand twice—
  And going—and gone," cried he;
The people cheered, but some of them cried,
  "We do not understand;
What changed its worth?" Quick came the reply,
  "The touch of a master's hand."

And many a man with life out of tune,
  And battered and scarred with sin,
Is auctioned cheap to a thoughtless crowd,
  Much like the old violin,
A mess of pottage—a glass of wine,
  A game—and he travels on;
He's going once—and going twice—
  He's going—and almost gone!
But the Master comes, and the foolish crowd
  Never can quite understand,
The worth of a soul, and the change that's wro't
  By the touch of the Master's hand.
  —*Myra Welch*

HE FAILETH NOT

Each happy morn when I awake,
This promise for the day I take:
"I'll never leave thee, nor forsake,"
  He faileth not!

Along life's road I'll fear no ill,
For Christ my Lord is with me still;
He never faileth! He never will!
  He faileth not!

He has not failed me in the past,
He will not fail while life shall last,
For wheresoe'er my lot be cast,
  He faileth not!

SUFFICIENCY

His grace is sufficient,
  Then why need I fear,
Though the testing be hard,
  And the trial severe?
He tempers each wind
  That upon me doth blow,
And tenderly whispers,
  "Thy Father doth know."

His pow'r is sufficient,
  Then why should I quail,
Though the storm clouds hang low,
  And though wild is the gale?
His strength will not falter,
  Whatever betide,
And safe on His bosom
  He bids me to hide.

His love is sufficient,
  Yea, boundless and free;
As high as the mountains,
  As deep as the sea.
Ah, there I will rest
  Till the darkness is o'er,
And wake in His likeness,
  To dwell evermore.

—*Avis B. Christiansen*

LOVE FOR ALL

God loved the world of sinners lost,
   And ruined by the fall.
Salvation full, at highest cost,
   He offers free to all.

Love brings the glorious fulness in,
   And to His saints makes known
The blessed rest from inbred sin,
   Through faith in Christ alone.
            —*Mrs. M. Stockton*

THE BEST CHOICE

He knows, He loves, He cares,
   Nothing this truth can dim,
He gives the very best to those
   Who leave the choice with Him.

HE GIVETH MORE

He giveth more grace when the burdens grow
      greater,
  He sendeth more strength when the labors
      increase;
To added affliction He addeth His mercy,
  To multiplied trials, His multiplied peace.

When we have exhausted our store of
      endurance,
  When our strength has failed ere the day is
      half done,
When we reach the end of our hoarded resources,
  Our Father's full giving is only begun.

His love has no limit, His grace has no measure,
  His power no boundary known unto men;
For out of His infinite riches in Jesus
  He giveth and giveth and giveth again.
                  —Annie Johnson Flint

WHEN I THINK OF HIS LOVE

When I think of the cross where my Saviour died,
  'Neath the frown of the darkened skies,
When I hear the groan of the Crucified,
  And I look on those death-closed eyes,
When I know that for me He the anguish bore,
  From sin He might set me free,
Oh, I know that I'll love Him forevermore,
  When I think of His love for me.

When I think of the grave where they laid my Lord,
  And they sealed Him within the gloom,
When I think how according to His Word,
  He arose from that vanquished tomb,
Oh, I know that for me He endured it all,
  My eyes with tears grow dim,
While low at His feet in love I fall,
  Whenever I think of Him.
          —*Louis Paul Lehman, Jr.*

GOD'S PAY

Who does God's work will get God's pay,
However long may be the day.
He does not pay as others pay,
In gold, or land, or raiment gay,
In goods that perish or decay;
But God's high wisdom knows the way,
And this is sure, let come what may—
Who does God's work will get God's pay.

GROWTH...

A THANKSGIVING

For all Thy blessings given there are many to thank
  Thee, Lord,
But for the gifts withholden I fain would add my
  word.
For the good things I desired that barred me from
  the best,
The peace at the price of honor, the sloth of a shame-
  ful rest;
The poisonous sweets I longed for to my hungering
  heart denied,
The staff that broke and failed me when I walked in
  the way of pride;
The tinsel joys withheld that so content might still be
  mine,
The help refused that might have made me loose my
  hand from Thine;
The light withdrawn that I might not see the dangers
  of my way;
For what Thou has not given, I thank Thee, Lord,
  today.

—*Annie Johnson Flint*

PRAYER AT EVENTIDE

For hasty word and secret sin
   For needful task undone,
We pray Thy full forgiveness, Lord,
   At setting sun.

The day to us has beauty brought,
   Thy smile has blessed our way,
Now as the evening hours come
   For rest we pray.

Keep us beneath Thy wings tonight
   Where peace alone is found,
For in Thy love we rest secure
   Thy arms around.

And when tomorrow's duties call,
   With joy or sorrow sown,
May we in full surrender seek
   Thy will alone. Amen.

              —*Bob Jones, Jr.*

LIFE'S JOY

God gives us joy that we may give;
   He gives us love that we may share;
Sometimes He gives us loads to lift
   That we may learn to bear.
For life is gladder when we give,
   And love is sweeter when we share,
And heavy loads rest lightly, too,
   When we have learned to bear.

A HEART THAT WEEPS

Oh, for a heart that weeps o'er souls,
  Weeps with a love in anguish born!
Oh, for a broken, contrite heart,
  A heart for sinners rent and torn!

Oh, for the pangs of Calv'ry's death,
  In fellowship with Thee, my Lord!
Oh, for the death that lives in life,
  And bleeds for those who spurn Thy Word!

Naught have I sought of blessing, Lord,
  Save that which brings lost souls to Thee;
All else is vain, nor dare I boast—
  This, Lord, I crave, be this my plea.

Have Thou Thy way whate'er the cost,
  In death I live, in life I die;
Thy way, not mine, dear Lord, I pray,
  Souls, precious souls, my ceaseless cry.
                    —*Oswald J. Smith*

A SURE PROMISE

In the common round of duty
  Lift thy heart in praise;
For the Lord hath surely promised
  Strength for all thy days.
                    —*Herbert G. Tovey*

73

REMEMBRANCE

I prayed, "Lord, take away the pain."
"Remember, child," He said, "the stain
Upon my Cross, the stain of red."
With quickening tears I hung my head.

"Oh, take away the sorrow, Lord,"
I prayed. "Remember, child, the sword
That pierced my heart," the Saviour said,
"When those I loved and trusted fled."
In deepest shame I hung my head.

At last I prayed, "Lord, sanctify
The suffering and grief." Then I
Knew the peace and joy, that I might share
Gethsemane; and lingering there,
I glimpsed beyond the darkened sod
The shining citadel of God.

—Grace V. Watkins

THE THREE PRAYERS

I.

"Lord, help me," so we pray,
   "Help me my work to do;
I am so ignorant and weak,
   Make me more wise and true."

II.

"Lord, help me to do Thy work,"
   We pray when wiser grown,
When on the upward way
   Our feet have farther gone.

III.

"Lord, do Thy work through me";
  So when all self we lose;
His doing and His work, and we
  The tools His hand can use.

—Annie Johnson Flint

BE STILL

Be still, my soul and listen,
For God would speak to thee,
And while the tempest's raging
Thy refuge He would be.

Be still, and cease to struggle,
Seek not to understand;
The flames will not destroy thee,
Thou'rt in the Father's hand.

And when the burden's heavy
He seeks to make thee pure,
To give thee faith and patience
And courage to endure.

The way is not too hard for thee,
Endure the chastening rod;
Thy gold shall only be refined,
Be still, submit to God.

—G. W. S.

MADE PERFECT THROUGH SUFFERING

I bless thee, Lord, for sorrows sent
    To break my dream of human power;
For now, my shallow cistern spent,
    I find thy founts, and thirst no more.

I take Thy hand, and fears grow still;
    Behold Thy face, and doubts remove;
Who would not yield his wavering will
    To perfect Truth and boundless Love?

That Love this restless soul doth teach
    The strength of thine eternal calm;
And tune its sad but broken speech
    To join on earth the angel's psalm.

Oh, be it patient in thy hands,
    And drawn, through each mysterious hour,
To service of thy pure commands,
    The narrow way of Love and Power.

—*Samuel Johnson*

CHRIST'S BONDSERVANT

Make me a captive, Lord,
   And then I shall be free;
Force me to render up my sword,
   And I shall conqueror be.
I sink in life's alarms
   When by myself I stand;
Imprison me within Thine arms,
   And strong shall be my hand.

My heart is weak and poor
   Until it master find;
It has no spring of action sure—
   It varies with the wind;
It cannot freely move
   Till Thou hast wrought its chain;
Enslave it with Thy matchless love,
   And deathless it shall reign.

My will is not my own
   Till Thou hast made it Thine;
If it would reach a monarch's throne
   It must its crown resign:
It only stands unbent
   Amid the clashing strife,
When on Thy bosom it has lent
   And found in Thee its life.

             —George Matheson

GROWING IN GRACE

Some of us stay at the cross,
  Some of us wait at the tomb,
Quickened and raised together with Christ,
  Yet lingering still in its gloom.
Some of us bide at the Passover feast
  With Pentecost all unknown;
The triumphs of grace in the heavenly place
  That our Lord has made our own.

If the Christ who died had stopped at the cross,
  His work had been incomplete;
If the Christ who was buried had stayed in the tomb,
  He had only known defeat.
But the way of the cross never stops at the cross,
  And the way of the tomb leads on
To the victorious grace in the heavenly place,
  Where the risen Lord has gone.
                                    —*Annie Johnson Flint*

(Copyright by Evangelical Publishers, Toronto, Canada.)

A SONG OF LOW DEGREE

He that is down need fear no fall;
  He that is low, no pride;
He that is humble ever shall
  Have God to be his guide.

I am content with what I have,
  Little be it or much;
And, Lord, contentment still I crave,
  Because thou savest such.

Fullness to such a burden is
  That go on pilgrimage;
Here little, and hereafter bliss,
  Is best from age to age.

                              —*John Bunyan*

NEW EVERY MORNING

Every day is a fresh beginning,
  Every morn is the world made new;
You who are weary of sorrow and sinning,
  Here is a beautiful hope for you—
  A hope for me and a hope for you.

All the past things are past and over,
  The tasks are done and the stars are shed;
Yesterday's errors let yesterday cover;
  Yesterday's wounds, which smarted and bled,
  Are healed with the healing which night has shed.

Yesterday is a part of forever,
  Bound up in a sheaf which God holds tight;
With glad days and sad days and bad days which never
  Shall visit us more with their bloom and their blight,
  Their fullness of sunshine or sorrowful night.

Let them go, since we cannot relieve them;
  Cannot undo, and cannot atone;
God in His mercy, receive, forgive them!
  Only the new days are our own.
  Today is ours, and today alone.

Here are the skies all burnished brightly,
  Here is the spent earth all reborn;
Here are the tired limbs springing lightly
  To face the sun, and to share with the morn
  In the prism of dew and the cool of dawn.

Every day is a fresh beginning;
  Listen, my soul, to the glad refrain,
And, spite of all sorrow and old sinning,
  And puzzle forecasted, and possible pain,
  Take heart with the day, and begin again.
  —*Susan Coolidge*

"IN A MOMENT"

A moment more and I may be
Caught up in glory, Lord, with Thee:
And, raptured sight, Thy beauty see
    For evermore!

A moment more—what joy to wear
Thy likeness, Saviour, and to share
With Thee the place prepared there,
    Where Thou art gone!

A moment more—upon Thy throne,
Thy place by right, then made our own;
Thou wilt not fill that seat alone,
    But with Thy saints!

SOWING AND REAPING

In spite of sorrow, loss, and pain,
  Our course be onward still;
We sow on Burma's barren plain,
  We reap on Zion's hill.
  —*Adoniram Judson*

HAPPY ANY WAY

Lord, it belongs not to my care
   Whether I die or live;
To love and serve Thee is my share,
   And this Thy grace must give.

If life be long, I will be glad
   That I may long obey;
If short, yet why should I be sad
   To soar to endless day?

Christ leads me through no darker rooms
   Than He went through before;
He that into God's kingdom comes
   Must enter by His door.

Come, Lord, when grace hath made me meet
   Thy blessed face to see;
For, if Thy work on earth be sweet,
   What will Thy glory be?

Then I shall end my sad complaints,
   And weary, sinful days,
And join with the triumphant saints
   Who sing Jehovah's praise.

My knowledge of that life is small;
   The eye of faith is dim;
But 'tis enough that Christ knows all,
   And I shall be with Him.

                 —*Richard Baxter*

ZEAL IN LABOR

Go, labor on; spend and be spent,
  Thy joy to do the Father's will;
It is the way the Master went;
  Should not the servant tread it still?

Go, labor on; 'tis not for naught;
  Thine earthly loss is heavenly gain;
Men heed thee, love thee, praise thee not;
  The Master praises — what are men?

Go, labor on; your hands are weak;
  Your knees are faint, your soul cast down;
Yet falter not; the prize you seek
  Is near—a kingdom and a crown!

Toil on, faint not; keep watch and pray!
  Be wise the erring soul to win;
Go forth into the world's highway;
  Compel the wanderer to come in.

Toil on, and in thy toil rejoice;
  For toil comes rest, for exile home;
Soon shalt thou hear the Bridegroom's voice
  The midnight peal, "Behold, I come!"

—Horatius Bonar

"QUITE SUDDENLY"

Quite suddenly — it may be at the turning of a lane,
Where I stand to watch a skylark from out the swelling grain,
That the trump of God shall thrill me, with its call so loud and clear,
And I'm called away to meet Him, whom of all I hold most dear.

Quite suddenly — it may be as I tread the busy street,
Strong to endure life's stress and strain, its every call to meet,
That through the roar of traffic, a trumpet, silvery clear,
Shall stir my startled senses and proclaim His Coming near.

Quite suddenly — it may be in His house I bend my knee,
When the kingly voice, long hoped for, comes at last to summon me;
And the fellowship of earth-life that has seemed so passing sweet,
Proves nothing but the shadow of our meeting round His feet.

Quite suddenly — it may be as I lie in dreamless sleep,
God's gift to many a sorrowing heart, with no more tears to weep,
That a call shall break my slumber and a Voice sound in my ear;
"Rise up, my love, and come away! Behold the Bridegroom's here!"

PRAYER...

BLESSINGS OF PRAYER

What various hindrances we meet
In coming to a mercy-seat!
Yet who that knows the worth of prayer
But wishes to be often there!

Prayer makes the darkened cloud withdraw;
Prayer climbs the ladder Jacob saw;
Gives exercise to faith and love;
Brings every blessing from above.

Restraining prayer, we cease to fight;
Prayer keeps the Christian's armor bright;
And Satan trembles when he sees
The weakest saint upon his knees.

Were half the breath that's vainly spent
To heaven in supplication sent,
Our cheerful song would oftener be
"Hear what the Lord has done for me."
                              —*William Cowper*

WHAT IS PRAYER?

Prayer is the soul's sincere desire,
 Uttered or unexpressed;
The motion of a hidden fire
 That trembles in the breast.

Prayer is the burden of a sigh,
 The falling of a tear,
The upward glancing of an eye,
 When none but God is near.

Prayer is the simplest form of speech
 That infant lips can try;
Prayer the sublimest strains that reach
 The Majesty on high.

Prayer is the contrite sinner's voice,
 Returning from his ways;
While angels in their songs rejoice
 And cry, "Behold, he prays!"

Prayer is the Christian's vital breath,
 The Christian's native air,
His watchword at the gates of death;
 He enters heaven with prayer.

O Thou, by whom we come to God,
  The Life, the Truth, the Way,
The path of prayer Thyself hast trod;
  Lord, teach us how to pray!

                    —*James Montgomery*

DO I REALLY PRAY?

I often say my prayers,
  But do I really pray?
And do the wishes of my heart
  Go with the words I say?

I may as well kneel down
  And worship gods of stone,
As offer to the living God
  A prayer of words alone.

For words without the heart
  The Lord will never hear;
Nor will He to those lips attend
  Whose prayer is not sincere!

Lord, show me what I need
  And teach me how to pray,
And help me when I seek Thy grace
  To mean the words I say.

                    —*John Burton*

ACCESSIBILITY OF PRAYER

The place of prayer is high enough
　To bring heaven's glory nigh,
And our need speaks clear to our Father's ear,
　And is open to His eye.

—*Annie Johnson Flint*

ENOUGH FOR ME

I am so weak, dear Lord, I cannot stand
   One moment without Thee;
But, oh, the tenderness of Thine enfolding!
And, oh, the faithfulness of Thine upholding!
And, oh, the strength of Thy right hand!
   That strength is enough for me.

I am so needy, Lord, and yet I know
   All fullness dwells in Thee;
And hour by hour, that never-failing treasure
Supplies and fills in overflowing measure,
My least and greatest need, and so
   Thy grace is enough for me.

It is so sweet to trust Thy Word alone.
   I do not ask to see
The unveiling of Thy purpose, or the shining
Of future light on mysteries untwining.
Thy promise-roll is all my own—
   Thy Word is enough for me.

                         —*Frances Ridley Havergal*

THE MYSTERIOUS WAY

God moves in a mysterious way
   His wonders to perform;
He plants His footsteps in the sea
   And rides upon the storm.

Deep in unfathomable mines
   Of never-failing skill,
He treasures up His bright designs
   And works His sovereign will.

Ye fearful saints, fresh courage take;
   The clouds ye so much dread
Are big with mercy, and shall break
   In blessings on your head.

Judge not the Lord by feeble sense,
   But trust Him for His grace;
Behind a frowning providence
   He hides a smiling face.

His purposes will ripen fast,
   Unfolding every hour;
The bud may have a bitter taste,
   But sweet will be the flower.

Blind unbelief is sure to err,
   And scan His work in vain;
God is His own interpreter,
   And He will make it plain.

—*William Cowper*

PROGRESS

Until I learned to trust
  I never learned to pray,
Nor did I learn to fully trust
  Till sorrows came my way.
Until I felt my weakness,
  His strength I never knew,
Nor dreamed till I was stricken
  That He could see me through.

When deepest drinks of sorrow,
  Drinks deepest too of grace;
He sends the storm so He Himself
  Can be our hiding place.
His heart, that seeks our highest good,
  Knows well when things annoy;
We would not long for heaven
  If earth held only joy!
                    —*Barbara C. Ryberg*

MY ALL

Not mine, not mine the choice
  In things or great or small;
Be Thou my guide, my strength,
  My wisdom and my all.
                    —*Horatius Bonar*

I CAN TRUST

I cannot see, with my small human sight,
Why God should lead this way or that for me;
I only know He saith, "Child, follow me."
    But I can trust.

I know not why my path should be at times
So straitly hedged, so strongly barred before;
I only know God could keep wide the door;
    But I can trust.

I find no answer, often, when beset
With questions fierce and subtle on my way,
And often have but strength to faintly pray;
    But I can trust.

I often wonder, as with trembling hand
I cast the seed along the furrowed ground,
If ripened fruit will in my life be found;
    But I can trust.

I cannot know why suddenly the storm
Should rage so fiercely round me in its wrath;
But this I know—God watches all my path,
    And I can trust.

I may not draw aside the mystic veil
That hides the unknown future from my sight;
Nor know if for me waits the dark or light;
    But I can trust.

I have no power to look across the tide,
To see, while here, the land beyond the river;
But this I know, I shall be God's forever;
　　　So, I can trust.

QUIETNESS

Be still and know that I am God,
That I who made and gave thee life
Will lead thy faltering steps aright;
That I who see each sparrow's fall
Will hear and heed thy earnest call.
　　　I am thy God!

Be still and know that I am God,
When aching burdens crush thy heart,
Then know I formed thee for thy part
And purpose in the plan I hold.
　　　Trust thou in God.

Be still and know that I am God,
Who made the atom's tiny span
And set it moving to My plan,
That I who guide the stars above
Will guide and keep thee in My love,
　　　For I am God!

—Doran

LORD, INCREASE MY FAITH

O for a faith that will not shrink
    Though pressed by many a foe,
That will not tremble on the brink
    Of poverty or woe.

That will not murmur nor complain
    Beneath the chastening rod,
But in the hour of grief or pain
    Can lean upon its God.

A faith that shines more bright and clear
    When tempests rage without,
That when in danger knows no fear,
    In darkness feels no doubt.

Lord, give me such a faith as this
    And then, whate'er may come,
I taste e'en now the hallowed bliss
    Of an eternal home.

CONFESSION

Last night my little boy confessed to me
Some childish wrong;
And kneeling at my knee
He prayed with tears—
"Dear God, make me a man
Like Daddy—wise and strong,
I know You can."

Then while he slept
I knelt beside his bed,
Confessed my sins,
And prayed with low-bowed head,
"O God, make me a child
Like my child here—
Pure, guileless,
Trusting Thee with faith sincere."

TOMORROW'S WAY

I know not if tomorrow's way
   Be steep or rough;
But when His hand is guiding me,
   That is enough.
And so, although the veil has hid
   Tomorrow's way,
I walk with perfect faith and trust,
   Through each today.

The love of God has hung a veil
   Around tomorrow.
That we may not its beauty see
   Nor trouble borrow.
But, oh, 'tis sweeter far, to trust
   His unseen hand,
And know that all the paths of life,
   His wisdom planned.

I WILL NOT DOUBT

I will not doubt, though all my ships at sea
Come drifting home with broken masts and sails;
I will believe the Hand which never fails
From seeming evil worketh good for me.
And though I weep because those sails are tattered,
Still will I cry, while my best hopes lie shattered;
I trust in Thee.

I will not doubt, though all my prayers return
Unanswered from the still, white realm above;
I will believe it is an all-wise love
Which has refused these things for which I yearn
And though at times I cannot keep from grieving,
Yet the pure ardor of my fixed believing
Undimmed shall burn.

I will not doubt, though sorrows fall like rain,
And troubles swarm like bees about a hive;
I will believe the heights for which I strive
Are only reached by anguish and by pain.
And though I groan and writhe beneath my crosses,
I yet shall see through my severest losses
The greater gain.

I will not doubt. Well anchored is this faith,
Like some staunch ship, my soul braves every gale;
So strong its courage that it will not quail
To breast the mighty unknown sea of death.
O, may I cry, though body parts with spirit,
I do not doubt, so listening worlds may hear it,
With my last **breath.**

"AS THOU GOEST, STEP BY STEP, I WILL OPEN UP THE WAY BEFORE THEE"

Child of My love, fear not the unknown morrow,
　　Dread not the new demand life makes of thee;
Thy ignorance doth hold no cause for sorrow
　　Since what thou knowest not is known to Me.

Thou canst not see today the hidden meaning
　　Of My command, but thou the light shalt gain;
Walk on in faith, upon My promise leaning,
　　And as thou goest all shall be made plain.

One step thou seest — then go forward boldly,
　　One step is far enough for faith to see;
Take that, and thy next duty shall be told thee,
　　For step by step thy Lord is leading thee.

Stand not in fear thy adversaries counting,
　　Dare every peril, save to disobey;
Thou shalt march on, all obstacles surmounting,
　　For I, the Strong, will open up the way.

Wherefore go gladly to the task assigned thee,
　　Having My promise, needing nothing more,
Than just to know, where'er the future find thee,
　　In all thy journeying I go before.

PERFECT PEACE

Like a river glorious is God's perfect peace;
Over all victorious in its bright increase;
Perfect, yet it floweth fuller every day,
Perfect, yet it groweth deeper all the way.

Hidden in the hollow of His blessed hand,
Never foe can follow, never traitor stand;
Not a surge of worry, not a shade of care,
Not a blast of hurry touch the spirit there.

Every joy or trial falleth from above,
Traced upon our dial by the Sun of Love,
We may trust Him fully, all for us to do;
They who trust Him wholly find Him wholly true.

—*Frances Ridley Havergal*

A SURE TRUST

Do not fear to claim His promise
    He will not your trust betray;
While on earth He healed them gladly,
    And He's just the same today.

A PERFECT FAITH

O for a faith that will not shrink
  Though pressed by every foe,
That will not tremble on the brink
  Of any earthly woe!

That will not murmur nor complain
  Beneath the chastening rod,
But in the hour of grief or pain
  Will lean upon its God;

A faith that shines more bright and clear
  When tempests rage without;
That when in danger knows no fear,
  In darkness feels no doubt;

That bears, unmoved, the world's dread frown,
  Nor heeds its scornful smile;
That seas of trouble cannot drown,
  Nor Satan's arts beguile.

Lord, give us such a faith as this,
  And then, whate'er may come,
We'll taste, e'en here, the hallowed bliss
  Of an eternal home.

—William H. Bathurst

DUSK FOR ME

Dusk for me, but when the shadows lengthen
  Know this, that in the shadows deep
God comes my faltering heart to strengthen
  And gently cradles me in sleep.

But such a dusk as falls o'er life's brief day
  Must in the morning vanish with the sun,
God will waken me to endless life I pray,
  When night at last is done.

Dusk for me, and the taps are sounding,
  And over hill and plain
From the silent dusk rebounding,
  Comes the death-call's sad refrain.

But God, who uses shades of night
  To veil the day's reborning,
Can change the taps that now affright
  Into the reveille of morning

Dusk for me, and may there be no tears
  When someday I have my leave-taking,
For God doth quiet all my fears,
  And the dawn — the dawn is breaking!
                —*Louis Paul Lehman, Jr.*

ALL THE WAY MY SAVIOUR LEADS ME

All the way my Saviour leads me;
What have I to ask beside?
Can I doubt His tender mercy,
Who through life has been my Guide?
Heavenly peace, divinest comfort,
Here by faith in Him to dwell!
For I know, whate'er befall me,
Jesus doeth all things well.

All the way my Saviour leads me,
Cheers each winding path I tread,
Gives me grace for every trial,
Feeds me with the living bread.
Though my weary steps may falter,
And my soul athirst may be,
Gushing from the Rock before me,
Lo! a spring of joy I see.

All the way my Saviour leads me;
Oh, the fullness of His love!
Perfect rest to me is promised
In my Father's house above.
When my spirit, clothed immortal,
Wings its flight to realms of day;
This my song thro' endless ages:
Jesus led me all the way.

—*Fanny J. Crosby*

DAY BY DAY

Charge not thyself with the weight of a year,
Child of the Master, faithful and dear:
Choose not the cross for the coming week,
For that is more than He bids thee seek.

Bend not thine arms for tomorrow's load;
Thou mayest leave that to thy gracious God.
"Daily," only He saith to thee,
"Take up thy cross and follow Me."

DWELL DEEP, MY SOUL

Dwell deep, my soul, dwell deep!
The little things that chafe and fret
  O waste not golden hours to give them heed!
The slight, the thoughtless wrong do thou forget;
  Be self-forgot in serving other's need
Thou faith in God through love for man shalt keep—
  Dwell deep, my soul, dwell deep!

WARNING...

HAVE YOU FORGOTTEN GOD?

In the glare of earthly pleasure,
In the fight for earthly treasure,
'Mid your blessings without measure—
    Have you forgotten God?

While His daily grace receiving,
Are you still His Spirit grieving
By a heart that's unbelieving—
    Have you forgotten God?

While His bounty you're accepting,
Are you His commands neglecting
And His call to you rejecting—
    Have you forgotten God?

IF I HAD KNOWN

I might have said a word of cheer
   Before I let him go.
His wistful eyes — they haunt me yet!
   But how could I foreknow
That slighted chance would be the last
   To me in mercy given?
Remorseful yearnings cannot send
   That word from earth to heaven.

I might have looked the love I felt;
   My brother had sore need
Of that for which, all shy and proud,
   He had not speech to plead.
But self is near, and self is strong,
   And I was blind that day!
He sought within my careless eyes
   And went athirst away.

O smile and clasp and word withheld!
   O brother-heart, now stilled!
Dear life, forever out of reach,
   I might have warmed and filled.
Talents misused and treasures lost
   O'er which I mourn in vain,
A waste as barren to my tears,
   As desert sands to rain!

Ah, friends! whose eyes today may hold
  Converse with living eyes,
Whose touch or tone or smile may thrill
  Sad souls with sweet surprise;
Be instant, like your Lord, with love
  And constant as His grace,
With dew and light and manna fall—
  The night comes on apace.
                    —*Mary Virginia Terhune*

THE CRITIC

A little seed lay on the ground,
And soon began to sprout;
"Now, which of all the flowers around,"
It mused, "shall I come out?
The lily's face is fair and proud,
But just a trifle cold;
The rose, I think, is rather loud,
And then, its fashion's old.
The violet is all very well,
But not a flower I'd choose;
Nor yet the Canterbury bell—
I never cared for blues."
And so it criticized each flower,
This supercilious seed,
Until it woke one summer morn,
And found itself — a weed.

BUILDING THE BRIDGE FOR HIM

An old man, traveling a lone highway,
Came at the evening cold and gray,
To a chasm deep and wide.

The old man crossed in the twilight dim,
For the sullen stream held no fears for him,
But he turned when he reached the other side,
And builded a bridge to span the tide.

"Old man," cried a fellow pilgrim near,
"You are wasting your strength with building here;
Your journey will end with the ending day,
And you never again will pass this way.

"You have crossed the chasm deep and wide.
Why build you a bridge at eventide?"
And the builder raised his old gray head:
"Good friend, on the path I have come," he said,
"There followeth after me today
A youth whose feet will pass this way.

"This stream, which has been as naught to me,
To that fair-haired boy may a pitfall be;
He, too, must cross in the twilight dim—
Good friend, I am building this bridge for him."

—*W. A. Dromgoole*

THE WATCHFUL SERVANT

Ye servants of the Lord,
Each in his office wait,
Observant of His Heavenly Word,
And watchful at His gate.

Let all your lamps be bright,
And trim the golden flame;
Gird up your loins, as in His sight,
For awful is His Name.

Watch: 'tis your Lord's command,
And while we speak He's near;
Mark the first signal of His hand,
And ready all appear.

Oh, happy servant he,
In such a posture found!
He shall his Lord with rapture see,
And be with honor crowned.

—*Philip Doddridge*

KINDNESS

Be swift, dear heart, in saying
     The kindly word;
When ears are sealed thy passionate pleading
     Will not be heard.

Be swift, dear heart, in doing
     The gracious deed;
Lest soon, they whom thou hold dearest
     Be past thy need.

THE CLOCK OF LIFE

The clock of life is wound but once,
And no man has the power
To tell just when the hands will stop,
At late or early hour.
Now is the only time you own;
Live, love, work, and with a will;
Place no faith in the morrow, for—
The clock may then be still.

INDEX BY AUTHOR

INDEX BY TITLE